Choosing to CHANGE

SHARON A. STEELE

Gospel Light

AGLOW.
INTERNATIONAL

D0033891

Gospel Light is an evangelical Christian publisher dedicated to serving the local church. We believe God's vision for Gospel Light is to provide church leaders with biblical, user-friendly materials that will help them evangelize, disciple and minister to children, youth and families.

We hope this Gospel Light resource will help you discover biblical truth for your own life and help you minister to adults. God bless you in your work.

For a free catalog of resources from Gospel Light please contact your Christian supplier or call 1-800-4-GOSPEL.

PUBLISHING STAFF
William T. Greig, Publisher
Dr. Elmer L. Towns, Senior Consulting Publisher
Dr. Gary S. Greig, Senior Consulting Editor
Jill Honodel, Editor
Pam Weston, Assistant Editor
Kyle Duncan, Associate Publisher
Bayard Taylor, M.Div., Editor, Theological and Biblical Issues
Barbara LaVan Fisher, Cover Designer
Debi Thayer, Designer
Eva Gibson, Contributing Writer

ISBN 0-8307-2131-2
© 1998 Sharon A. Steele
All rights reserved.
Printed in U.S.A.

Aglow International is an interdenominational organization of Christian women. Our mission is to lead women to Jesus Christ and provide opportunity for Christian women to grow in their faith and minister to others.

Our publications are used to help women find a personal relationship with Jesus Christ, to enhance growth in their Christian experience, and to help them recognize their roles and relationships according to Scripture.

For more information about our organization, please write to Aglow International, P.O. Box 1749, Edmonds, WA 98020-1749, U.S.A., or call (425) 775-7282. For ordering or information about the Aglow studies, call (800) 793-8126.

CONTENTS

FOREWORD

When the apostle Paul poured out his heart in letters to the young churches in Asia, he was responding to his apostolic call to shepherd those tender flocks. They needed encouragement in their new lives in Jesus. They needed solid doctrine. They needed truth from someone who had an intimate relationship with God and with them.

Did Paul know as he was writing that these simple letters would form the bulk of the New Testament? We can be confident that the Holy Spirit did! How like God to use Paul's relationship with these churches to cement His plan and purpose in their lives and, generations later, in ours.

We in Aglow can relate to Paul's desire to bond those young churches together in the faith. After 1967, when Aglow fellowships began bubbling up across the United States and in other countries, they needed encouragement. They needed to know the fullness of who they were in Christ. They needed relationship. Like Paul, our desire to reach out and nurture from far away birthed a series of Bible studies that have fed thousands since 1973 when our first study, *Genesis*, was published. Our studies share heart-to-heart, giving Christians new insights about themselves and their relationships with and in God.

God's generous nature has recently provided us a rewarding new relationship with Gospel Light Publications. Together we are publishing our Aglow classics, as well as a selection of exciting new studies. Gospel Light began as a publishing ministry much in the same way Aglow began publishing Bible studies. Henrietta Mears, one of its visionary founders, formed Gospel Light in response to requests from churches across America for the Sunday School materials she had written for the First Presbyterian Church in Hollywood, California. Gospel Light remains a strong ministry-minded witness for the gospel around the world.

Our hearts' desire is that these studies will continue to kindle the minds of women and men, touch their hearts and refresh spirits with the light and life a loving Savior abundantly supplies.

This study, *Choosing to Change* by Sharon Steele, shows you how to allow the Holy Spirit to renew your mind by building the attitudes of Christ into your thinking and transforming your life. I know its contents will reward you richly.

Jane Hansen
International President
Aglow International

INTRODUCTION

A woman sits across the table from you. "I want to see Christ's character repro-duced in my life," she confides. "But I don't know how to do it."

Her eyes fill with tears. "Every day it's the same old story, 'Lord, I've failed again.' Over and over, day after day. Can God really change my thoughts and transform my life? And if He can, what is my responsibility? I'd really like to know."

If you can identify at all with this woman, this Bible study is for you. Even though you are given a new nature when you become a child of God, change is not automatic. Using the comparison of our human minds to that of a com-puter, you will discover key truths that will show you how to let God change you into His likeness. Just as people have learned to use computers as tools to accomplish tasks quickly and efficiently, so can we learn to control our thoughts by allowing God to renew our minds. Through the power of the Holy Spirit we can find the power to live godly lives.

When we do not allow God to transform our thought patterns, we experi-ence confusion and frustration. Faulty thinking produces undesirable results in every area. Just as computers with defective programs must be repro-grammed before they can function effectively, so we must allow God to repro-gram our thinking and bring our thoughts under His control.

This study will show how you can allow the Holy Spirit to renew your mind, build the attitudes of Christ into your thinking and transform your life.

AN OVERVIEW OF THE STUDY

This Bible study is divided into four sections:

- **A CLOSER LOOK AT THE PROBLEM** defines the problem and the goal of the study.

- **A CLOSER LOOK AT GOD'S TRUTH** gets you into God's Word. What does God have to say about the problem? How can you begin to apply God's Word as you work through each lesson?
- **A CLOSER LOOK AT MY OWN HEART** will help you clarify and further apply truth. It will also give guidance as you work toward change.
- **ACTION STEPS I CAN TAKE TODAY** is designed to help you concentrate on immediate steps of action.

You Will Need

- A Bible.
- A notebook. During this study you will want to keep a journal to record what God shows you personally. You may also want to journal additional thoughts or feelings that come up as you go through the lessons. Some questions may require more space than is given in this study book.
- Time to meditate on what you're learning. You will also be encouraged to find a memory partner to work with you on memorizing Scripture. Giving the Holy Spirit time to personalize His Word for your heart will help you allow Him to renew your mind and transform your life.

HOW TO START AND LEAD
A SMALL GROUP

One key to starting and leading a small group is to ask yourself, What would Jesus do and how would he do it? Jesus began His earthly ministry with a small group of disciples. The fact of His presence made wherever He was a safe place to be. Think of a small group as a safe place. It is a place that reflects God's heart, God's hands. The way in which Jesus lived and worked with His disciples is a basic small group model that we are able to draw both from direction and nurture.

Paul exhorts us to "walk in love, as Christ also has loved us and given Himself for us" (Ephesians 5:2, *NKJV*). We, as His earthly reflections, are privileged to walk in His footsteps, to help bind up the brokenhearted as He did or simply to listen with a compassionate heart. Whether you use this book as a Bible study, or as a focus point for a support group, a church or home group, walking in love means that we "bear one another's burdens" (Galatians 6:2, *NKJV*). The loving atmosphere provided by a small group can nourish, sustain and lift us up as nothing else does.

Jesus walked in love and spoke from an honest heart. In His endless well of compassion He never misplaced truth. Rather, he surrounded it with mercy. Those who left His presence felt good about themselves because Jesus used truth to point them in the right direction for their lives. When He spoke about the sinful woman who washed Jesus' feet with her tears and wiped them with her hair, He did not deny her sin. He said, "her sins, which are many, are forgiven, for she loved much" (Luke 7:47, *NKJV*). That's honesty without condemnation.

Jesus was a model of servant leadership. "Whoever desires to become great among you shall be your servant. And whoever of you desires to be first shall be slave of all" (Mark 10:43,44, *NKJV*). One of the key skills a group leader possesses is to be able to encourage the group members to grow spiritually. Keeping in personal contact with each member of the group, especially if one is absent, tells each one that he/she is important to the group. Other skills an effective group leader will develop are: being a good listener, guiding the discussion, and guiding the group to deal with any conflicts that arise within it.

Whether you're a veteran or brand new to small group leadership, virtually every group you lead will be different in personality and dynamics. The constant is the presence of Jesus Christ, and when He is at the group's center, everything else can come together.

YOU'RE INVITED!

To grow...

> *To develop and reach maturity; thrive; to spring up; come into existence from a source;*

with a group

> *An assemblage of persons gathered or located together; a number of individuals considered together because of similarities;*

To explore...

> *To investigate systematically; examine; search into or range over for the purpose of discovery;*

new topics

> *Subjects of discussion or conversation.*

Meeting on

Date _____ Time_____

Located at

Place _____

_____

Contact _____

Phone _____

Note: Feel free to fill in this page and photocopy it as an invitation to hand out or post on your church bulletin board. © 1998 by Gospel Light. Permission to photocopy granted. *Choosing to Change.*

One

THE PROBLEM AND THE POTENTIAL: THE NEED FOR RENEWED MINDS

Computers with defective programs produce garbled, meaningless messages. In much the same way, believers with unspiritual minds produce similar confusing messages.

When we try to produce godly character with an unrenewed mind, we find ourselves puzzled by our ungodly actions. And that isn't all. Others watching us will be confused, too.

Allowing God's Spirit to reprogram our way of thinking means we will send out clear messages of His love and power to change lives. Renewed minds will produce godly character. This week's study will help us examine God's ideal of Christlike thinking and attitudes.

A Closer Look at the Problem

Minds that have not been renewed by the love and power of Jesus Christ are like computers that have not been plugged in. Regardless of their potential, computers are unable to function without sources of power. In the same way, people who have not received Jesus will never achieve God's plan for their lives.

1. What do the following verses teach about the natural mind?

Genesis 6:5

Colossians 1:21

THE HEART OF THE PROBLEM

The word "heart" in Scripture usually refers to the innermost being of a person, the seat of emotions, knowledge and wisdom. It is often used as a synonym for mind.

2. Read Ephesians 4:17-19. List the phrases that describe the minds and hearts of unbelievers.

What are the results of their way of thinking?

What are the results of a hardened heart?

When we accept Christ as Savior, much of our thinking is made new. God's Holy Spirit gives us new desires and perspectives. We now have a new Master Programmer who makes dramatic changes in our thinking.

Unfortunately, not all our thinking is made new at once. Scientists tell us that our minds collect data even before birth. The memories and thought patterns we store in our memory banks remain basically the same and have tremendous power.

In addition, our sinful natures that once controlled our minds still influence our thoughts and desires. Ungodly thoughts and memories haunt us, often causing great struggles with temptation.

God wants to help us overcome these old thought patterns. The goal of this lesson is to help us understand that His Spirit is available to reprogram our defective thinking with godly attitudes. This will result in peace and joy. Refusing to allow His Spirit the freedom to change our thinking will result in frustration and turmoil.

A Closer Look at God's Truth

3. Read Matthew 5:27-30. What did Jesus teach about sin and the thought life?

About the sources of temptation?

Jesus identified ungodly thoughts as sin which in turn cause sinful actions that destroy. The severity of His illustrations demonstrates the importance of dealing with sources of temptation.

How can you apply these verses to things that influence your mind, such as reading materials, television, videos, movies and the worldwide web?

What influences lead you to think sinful thoughts?

How can you eliminate or decrease their influence on your thinking?

4. Read Mark 7:20-23. What did Jesus identify as the origin of things that make one unclean?

What comes from the heart?

Every sin we commit begins in our minds. We may hide our thoughts and feelings, but eventually they come out in our actions. Trying to change our actions without allowing God to change our thought patterns results in failure.

5. What do the following passages show about the power of the mind?

Luke 6:43-45

Romans 12:2

We have desperate needs, therefore God has commanded us to be renewed in our minds. He also knows the struggles we have with our thoughts. We may hide them from others, but we cannot hide them from Him. However, we can choose to allow Him to make our thoughts pleasing to Him.

6. Read Philippians 2:1-11. What attitudes did the apostle Paul encourage in the lives of the Philippian believers (see vv. 2-4)?

What does verse 5 encourage us to develop?

How is Christ's attitude described (see vv. 6-8)?

How do Jesus' actions and attitudes contrast with those described in the first part of verse 3?

By nature, we are selfish. Programmed to desire power, recognition and prominence, we want to get ahead at the expense of others.

Jesus' attitude was a total contrast. He left the prominence and power of equality with God to become a humble servant and to die a criminal's death. Only a loving and giving mind could produce such self-sacrificing actions. It is this mind and attitude that the Holy Spirit wants to develop within us.

What attitude is encouraged in the last part of verse 3?

7. Read Mark 10:35-45. What did James and John request from Jesus?

Why do you think they made this request?

James and John expected Jesus to become king of Israel. In that day, sitting beside the king implied authority next to that of the ruler himself. How did the other apostles react to James's and John's request?

Why do you think they felt that way?

Describe how you would have felt if you had been one of the apostles.

How does the world measure greatness (see v. 42)?

What is the measure of greatness in Christ's kingdom?

How is Jesus an example of true greatness?

How does this passage demonstrate the difference between the natural mind and the mind renewed by Christ?

8. Read John 13:3-5,12-17. What did Jesus know (see v. 3)?

What servant's action did Jesus perform?

What had His disciples called Him (see v. 13)?

What was Jesus' reaction to those titles?

What can you learn about the mind of Christ from this passage?

We often seek to exalt ourselves to demonstrate our personal value. But Jesus had no questions about His worth. He knew exactly who He was and chose not to exalt Himself. Instead He humbled Himself and served others. The Christ-like mind expresses itself in similar actions.

List phrases that encourage a servant's attitude (see vv. 14-16):

Jesus took the role of a servant to meet a need of that day. What actions might He perform if He were physically on earth today?

How can you let Him perform those actions through you?

9. Read Romans 8:29. What is God's plan for you?

How would you describe a Christian whose life is conforming to the likeness of Jesus?

In our own human strength, we can never conform to His likeness. Regardless of our desires, we cannot make ourselves act like Jesus. But as we give the Holy Spirit freedom to work in our lives, He will develop qualities of Jesus within us.

10. Read Romans 12:1,2. To what are we not to conform?

What are we to be instead?

How does this happen?

A Closer Look at My Own Heart

BECOMING LIKE JESUS

The Greek word that has been translated "transformed" is *metamorphoo*. The English word "metamorphosis" comes from the same root. The Greek verb is in a passive tense, indicating that the transformation is done by another.

This is significant; we cannot transform ourselves. Only the Holy Spirit can renew our minds and transform our lives. Just as God changes a caterpillar into a butterfly through metamorphosis, so He can transform us from conformity to the world to the likeness of Jesus (see Romans 8:29).

This inner transformation by the Holy Spirit results in change.

11. Read 2 Corinthians 3:17,18. What is God's plan for you?

What phrases imply a continuing process?

Who is the source of this transformation?

It is easy for us to become overwhelmed with our weaknesses and failures. We want instant maturity and instant transformation into Jesus' likeness.

Renewed minds and transformed lives are not instantaneous nor are they totally achieved in this life. Paul recognized that "being transformed" is a process and takes time. It is by the power of the Holy Spirit that we are able to keep moving toward these goals.

12. Read the following verses. What is promised to those with renewed minds and hearts?

Isaiah 26:3

Romans 8:6

1 Thessalonians 3:13

The benefits of a renewed mind and heart are available to you as you submit to the lordship of Jesus. When you do, the Holy Spirit can purify your thoughts, renew your mind and give you the attitudes of Jesus.

Action Steps I Can Take Today

13. Ask God to show you specific ways that you can work with Him to build the thoughts and attitudes of Jesus into your mind. Record in your journal what He reveals to you.

14. You can change your life to become more Christlike by filling your mind with His Word. One of the best ways you can do this is by making a commitment to memorize Scripture. What you put in your mind is what you become!

    Find someone who has a commitment to memorizing Scripture and ask that person to be your partner. Call each other several times each week and repeat your verses to each other. When necessary, prompt each other and correct each other's mistakes. This can be done over the phone. You can also pray for one another.

    Understanding Scripture is essential for memorization. Write Romans 12:2 on a 3x5-inch card. Then turn it over and rewrite the verse in your own words on the back. Put your card where you can see it every day; it could be in your purse or wallet, on the dashboard of your car or by the bathroom sink. Each morning ask God to show you what it means and how He wants to make it real in your life that day. Share what you're learning with your memory partner when you review your verses together.

- Two -

Step One: Draw Near to God— Connect to the Power Source

Recently, I entered several pages of material on my computer. When finished, I decided to print what I had written. I carefully lined up the paper and hit all the right keys. Nothing happened. The printer did not budge. The electrical cord was plugged in. The potential for power was there, but the printer did not work.

Then I discovered that the cord connecting the computer to the printer had come loose. The printer was not on-line with the source of information. It could not print until the cord between the computer and the printer was firmly reconnected.

A Closer Look at the Problem

"ON-LINE" OR "OFF-LINE"?

In much the same way, Christians have tremendous potential when they are *on-line* with their power source. Sometimes, though, they get *off-line*. Instead of seeking the Lord first, they allow the distractions of this life to unsettle them. Instead of becoming strong in faith, they flounder and begin to make excuses for sinful attitudes and motives.

Yes, we often try to change our attitudes, thoughts and actions in our own strength and fail. We discover that even though we long to be more like Christ, desire alone is not enough to transform us.

The first step to the renewal of our minds is to develop a closer relationship with our Lord. Only when we are connected to His mighty power can old thought patterns change into new ones.

This lesson will show you how to keep *on-line* with Jesus, the author and perfecter of your faith (see Hebrews 12:2). If you have somehow gotten *off-line*, you will also discover how to get back on. And if you have never gotten on in the first place, you will discover how to connect with Him and receive new life in Christ.

A Closer Look at God's Truth

1. Read Proverbs 2:1-8. What does the Lord instruct us to do in verse 1?

    What phrase shows the importance of listening (see v. 2)?

    What phrase shows the need to seek new minds (see v. 2)?

    What phrases tell us to ask for wisdom (see v. 3)?

    How does verse 4 tell us to seek for wisdom?

What do verses 1 through 4 show you about your responsibility in receiving a renewed mind?

Too often, our time and energy is invested in securing lovely homes and other possessions. The writer of Proverbs, however, urges us to search for godly wisdom as one would search for silver hidden in a field. Continual, diligent effort is necessary to dig out this treasure. How much time and effort are you willing to invest in your search for godly wisdom?

What is the promised result (see Proverbs 2:5) of diligent effort to find godly wisdom?

What does verse 6 tell us about the source of godly thinking?

What does it mean to understand the fear of the Lord and to find the knowledge of God (see v. 5)?

Understanding the fear of the Lord means to have a deep reverence for Him. To find the knowledge of God implies knowing Him personally. If we want to grow in our understanding of His nature we must spend time with Him.

2. What do the following verses teach about receiving wisdom?

Psalm 25:8,9

Psalm 51:6

Proverbs 9:10

Just as computers will not work without being connected to sources of power, our mind will not be renewed without being connected to God. He is our ultimate source of power, wisdom and understanding. In the following passages, the apostle Paul draws the same conclusion.

3.   Read Colossians 1:24-29. What mystery has God revealed (see v. 27)?

What phrase identifies Paul's source of power (see v. 29)?

What does verse 29 reveal about this power?

Describe what is meant by the phrase "Christ in you, the hope of glory" (v. 27).

How did Paul's actions help others develop renewed minds (see v. 28)?

What is your responsibility in receiving a renewed mind?

GROWING UP IN CHRIST

Paul proclaimed a vital relationship with Christ as our only hope of victory and eternal glory. He dedicated all his energy to proclaiming the hope we have in Jesus. He taught and admonished his converts that he might present them mature in Christ.

After receiving Jesus as our Savior, we should allow His Spirit to work in us. We should also listen to godly teachers who challenge, exhort and strengthen us.

4.   Read Colossians 2:1-10. What result did Paul desire for believers (see v. 2)?

What does verse 3 teach about wisdom?

What are we instructed to do in verses 6 and 7?

What actions will help you become rooted and built up in Jesus?

Tree roots go deep into the ground to draw nourishment. Once they become firmly established, they will not be easily uprooted by storms. To be rooted in Jesus means we spend quality time with Him. Anything less will result in shallow roots that give way in the storms of life.

A Closer Look at My Own Heart

5.   Read Jeremiah 17:9. How does God describe the heart of the natural person?

Satan is not the only deceiver. Our hearts are deceptive, too. Because of this, we are slow to recognize our sinful attitudes and motives. Instead, we excuse them. We cannot always trust our consciences to be our guides.

6.   Read 1 Chronicles 28:9. What does this verse reveal to you about God's knowledge of your thoughts and motives?

Only God fully understands our motives. Inviting Him to examine us and make us aware of our sins helps us see what needs to be changed. As we confess those sins and ask for His forgiveness, He cleanses us. The result is a renewed mind.

As Jesus prepared His disciples for His impending death, He promised to send His Holy Spirit to enable them—and us—to live holy lives.

7. Read John 16:5-16. List words and phrases that describe the work of the Holy Spirit.

The Holy Spirit is the source of the renewed mind. The Spirit produces holy attitudes and actions, convicts of sin and guides into truth. When you allow the Holy Spirit freedom to work in you, He exerts His power so that you bring glory to Jesus. In turn, you willingly submit yourself to His leadership.

8. You can bring glory to Jesus by doing the following:
    Ask the Lord to reveal any hidden sins in your heart. After confessing them, ask Him to cleanse you, renew your mind and change your attitudes. Then pray Psalm 51:10: "Create in me a pure heart, O God, and renew a steadfast spirit within me."

Action Steps I Can Take Today

9. If you have never accepted Jesus as your personal Savior and Lord, you are invited to do so right now. Write a prayer paraphrasing the following verses: John 3:16; Romans 3:23; 5:8; 1 John 1:9; John 1:12. Ask Him to make you His child.

Make this truth your own right now: *God will change my way of thinking as I surrender control of my life to Him!*

Claim this verse as your own: "He who began a good work in you will carry it on to completion until the day of Christ Jesus" (Philippians 1:6).

10. If you have accepted Christ, use these questions to help you evaluate where you are right now in your relationship with your Lord.

    a. Are you walking daily in the fullness of His Holy Spirit?

    b. Will you ask His Spirit to fill and empower you afresh?

11. If you answered yes to questions 10a and 10b, you are next encouraged to evaluate the time you devote to building a relationship with the Lord.
    a. In your journal, make a list of things that are hindrances in your relationship with God. Ask Him to show you steps to eliminate these hindrances. Write these down.
    b. Now write down ways you can strengthen your personal relationship with God. Do you need to increase your time reading His Word and praying? Do you need to spend more time memorizing Scripture?
    c. Ask a friend to keep you accountable for the steps of action you have chosen to implement today.

12. Memorize Psalm 51:10. To help you remember this verse, picture it in your mind. Imagine that you are looking at a photograph of what the verse is about. What does a pure heart look like? A steadfast spirit? Share your picture with your memory partner when you recite the verse. Be sure to review Romans 12:2.

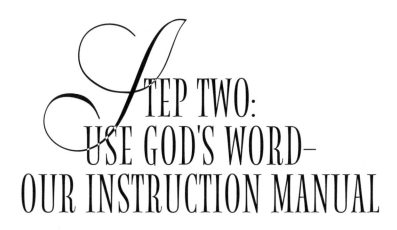

- *Three* -

*A*TEP TWO: USE GOD'S WORD– OUR INSTRUCTION MANUAL

The information a computer produces is directly related to what is entered into its memory. If I enter a misspelled word or inaccurate figures, these errors will be reproduced in subsequent data. If we input inaccurate information, it will be impossible for the computer to produce valid data.

A Closer Look at the Problem

THE SOURCE OF TRUTH

The human mind works much the same way. We cannot enter false information into our minds and expect our lives to demonstrate the truth of God. Inaccurate statements such as "God can't use me now," "I can't overcome this sin" or "I have no value" cause sinful actions, not truth and purity.

What is produced in our lives is directly related to what we put into our minds. If we want to demonstrate godly characteristics, we need to enter accurate information. The Bible is one source of information that can always be trusted to be correct. God's Word is truth. When we put it into our minds, it will make a difference in our attitudes and actions.

Although you have already been encouraged to memorize God's Word as a part of renewing your mind, this chapter will show you even more about the scriptural importance of allowing God's thoughts to become your thoughts; His desires, your desires; His attitudes, your attitudes. You will consider additional practical suggestions that will help you store God's Word in your mind so that its powerful influence can bring truth and accuracy into your thinking.

A Closer Look at God's Truth

1. Read Psalm 119. What results of reading and applying God's Word are found in the following verses?

   verses 9-11

   verse 28

   verse 40

   verses 99,100

   verse 164

2. List phrases from the following verses which imply memorizing Scripture:

   verse 11

verse 15

verse 61

The psalmist recognized the powerful influence of God's Word. Because he had hidden it deep in his heart, he personally knew the tremendous power of Scripture to change a life.

3.   What is promised to one who meditates upon God's Word?

Joshua 1:7,8

Psalm 1:2,3

How does the dictionary define the word "meditate"?

What do you think it means to meditate on God's Word?

Why is this important?

When we meditate on God's Word, we think about it, ponder it. We ask the Lord to give us new depths of understanding. "What does this passage mean? What does it mean to me? How can I apply this to my life?" Scriptural truth then becomes part of our thinking.

4. Read Matthew 4:1-11. The story of Jesus' temptation in the wilderness is an example of the power of God's Word to give strength to overcome sin. What phrase repeated in verses 4, 7 and 10 shows that Jesus used Scripture to fight Satan's temptations?

Since Jesus knew God's Word, He was able to use it to protect Himself from sin. We too can have this same protection as we study and meditate on Scripture. God's Word is powerful. We need to take it seriously.

5. The example of Eve being deceived in the Garden of Eden illustrates the danger of not taking God's Word seriously. Read 2 Corinthians 11:3,4,13-15. How was Eve deceived (see v. 3)?

What did Paul fear might happen to the Corinthian believers?

What were the Corinthians allowing?

How is Satan described in verse 14?

How are his servants described in verse 15?

What does this passage teach you about Satan and his tactics?

We need to be aware that Satan presents subtle temptations. What he offers appears good, sometimes even spiritual. It is important that we test all teaching by God's Word before we accept it.

6. Read Genesis 2:16,17; 3:1-7,13. What phrases from Genesis 3:1 show that Satan tried to make Eve doubt God's word?

How do Satan's words contradict God's in 2:17?

How did Satan make the temptation seem spiritually helpful?

What answer did Eve give when asked why she had disobeyed?

How did doubting God's word lead to Eve's sin?

Satan is a liar who tries to deceive us. But God's truth as recorded in His Word can become such a part of our minds that we can instantly recognize Satan's lies when we hear them. If Eve had tested words according to what God had said, she could have recognized the lie and been kept from sinning. Rejecting Scripture leads to sin. Accepting and obeying it leads to godliness.

7. Read Hebrews 4:12. How does this verse describe the Word of God?

What phrase shows the power of God's Word on the mind?

Give examples of how God's Word has revealed ungodly thoughts and attitudes in your life.

CHECK YOUR INFORMATION SOURCE

A friend of mine took a college course on computers. During her first hands-on lab, her instructor came to class without proper preparation. Instructions were given on how to accomplish a certain task, but some of the directions were incorrect and the task could not be accomplished. The flustered instructor gave further directions. These too failed. She turned to a book. Confused, she picked up the programming text instead of the computer manual. Once again she failed to give the right instructions.

Like that teacher, we too, are sometimes inadequately prepared and seek answers from the wrong source. However, the Bible is our only reliable manual for Christian living. It should be the first place we turn when we need help.

8. Read Acts 17:11. For what were the Berean believers commended?

The Bereans were commended because they not only received Paul's message with great eagerness, they searched the Scriptures daily to make certain that Paul was teaching the truth. They were eager to learn, but they refused to be gullible and accept what was not of God.

Too often, we can be led astray when we blindly follow powerful speakers with charisma. We need to test all teaching and prophetic utterances by Scripture, regardless of how important or spiritual the teachers seem to be. *Any teaching that does not line up with Scripture should not be accepted as coming from God.*

9. Read 2 Timothy 3:14-17. What does verse 16 teach about the source of Scripture?

What is the Word of God able to accomplish?

How are the results of studying God's Word related to the renewing of the mind?

If we want to be used of God in ministry, we must be prepared and equipped. Often we attempt to prepare ourselves by attending school, seminars, worship services and inspirational gatherings. While these are helpful, they are not a substitute for personal study of God's Word.

Why do you think this is so?

10. What do the following passages teach about the power of Scripture?

Mark 12:24

Romans 15:4

A Closer Look at My Own Heart

STORING GOD'S WORD IN YOUR MEMORY

One of the first lessons I learned when using a computer was the importance of the *Save* key. One day, after entering ten pages of material, a brief power outage erased it all. I had failed to save it in the memory bank. A simple push of the *Save* key at the end of each page would have recorded the information for easy recall.

When God created mankind, He equipped us with a save device—our memory. We can memorize Scripture and have it ready whenever we need it—strength in times of temptation, hope in despair and peace in chaos. It gives wisdom in decision making and guidance in counseling others. It reveals sin so we can be cleansed and forgiven. As we store God's Word in our memory banks, His thoughts and attitudes replace ours.

We often fail to memorize Scripture because we think we don't have time. But we all have wasted moments. When God impressed on me the importance of Scripture memorization, I asked Him to show me time in which to do it. I wrote verses on index cards and memorized them in the mornings as I curled my hair. Soon I was memorizing and reviewing while I waited for traffic lights, when I folded clothes, walked or rode my exercise bike. In less than a year, I had memorized over eighty verses.

What about you? Are there times in your schedule when you can store His Word in your memory? Ask Him to show them to you.

Action Steps I Can Take Today

11. Review the questions in this lesson. Note the results promised to those who read and study God's Word. Place a check mark by those results that you desire to see increase in your life.

12. Evaluate your schedule. For several days, keep track of wasted moments in your journal. At the end of the week prayerfully note what you've jotted down. Are there moments you could use to read the Scriptures or spend time going over the verses you've memorized? Share your discoveries with your memory partner. Then pray together about making a commitment to God to spend those moments in the Word.

13. Practice Scripture meditation by choosing either Deuteronomy 11:18,19 or a verse from this week's study that was especially meaningful to you. Ponder the questions: "What does this passage mean? What does it mean to me? How can I apply this to my life?" Make the verse more truly yours by writing it in your own words in your journal.

14. Meditating on specific verses is a valuable aid in Scripture memorization. Commit the verse you choose to memory. Review it several times each day this week. Share it with your memory partner. Both of you will grow as scriptural truth becomes an integral part of your thinking.

- Four -

STEP THREE: THINK ON GOOD THINGS– INPUT VALID DATA

A message on a bumper sticker states: "To err is human. To really foul things up takes a computer."

Computers get blamed for numerous errors, but many of the charges are unfounded. Programmers explain the situation with the acronym "GIGO" which means "garbage in, garbage out." Computers producing faulty data are usually doing exactly what they have been told to do. Either they were poorly programmed in the first place or fed faulty data later.

A Closer Look at the Problem

GARBAGE INPUT RESULTS IN GARBAGE OUTPUT
This is also true of our human minds. We get frustrated at our sinful thoughts, words and actions. But are we eating mental garbage? We cannot produce godliness when we fill our minds with trash.

1. Read 1 John 2:15-17. What are we instructed to avoid loving?

    What things come from the world (see v. 16)?

    How do you think living in an ungodly world influences your thinking?

Although we are not of the world, we are still in the world (see John 17:14-18). As a result, we receive stimulation toward ungodly thinking. Much of what we see and hear from the mass media and those around us encourage worldly and sensual thinking.

However, we choose whether or not to allow the world to affect our thinking. We choose what we put into our minds, and everything we put in influences our thoughts. If we want godly attitudes and actions, we must choose to think about good things.

This chapter will show us the importance of focusing our minds upon that which is good and wholesome. If "garbage in, garbage out" is true, then so is "God's Word in, godly actions out."

God's Word shows us we can have renewed minds.

2. For the next few days, record in your journal different sources of information that you feed into your mind. List radio programs, tapes, TV shows, movies, information from the internet, books, magazines, conversations and meetings.

    Note the approximate length of time you engage in each activity. Then make evaluations on the basis of whether it will strengthen or weaken your resolve toward godliness. Ask yourself, "Does this activity appeal to my sensual nature or does it draw me closer to God?"

A Closer Look at God's Truth

3. The Israelites struggled with temptations similar to the ones we struggle against. Although they had seen miracle after miracle of God's provision

and protection, they still turned away from Him. According to 1 Corinthians 10:1-10, what was their downfall?

4. Read Romans 8:5. Upon what does the sinful mind focus?

   Upon what does the spiritual mind focus?

   Upon whom are we instructed to focus?

It is vital to recognize that we can choose the direction of our thinking—on earthly or heavenly things. As we focus on spiritual things, we grow in our ability to let God's Spirit control our lives.

5. Read Galatians 6:7,8. What does a person reap?

   What is the result of sowing to please our sinful natures?

   What is the result of sowing to please the Holy Spirit?

   How does the principle of sowing and reaping apply to your thought life?

   What kinds of seeds are you planting?

If you want to grow carrots, you don't plant cucumber seeds, hoping they will grow into carrots. Only carrot seeds produce carrots.

Likewise, what you plant in your mind is exactly what you will reproduce in your life.

THE STRUGGLE OF THE OLD AGAINST THE NEW

An elderly man, who became a Christian late in life, struggled with sinful thoughts and temptations. One day, while talking to his pastor, he said, "I feel like I have two big dogs fighting inside me. One dog wants me to do evil; the other one wants me to do good."

"Which dog wins?" the pastor asked.

"The one I feed," the old man replied.

The nature we feed will grow stronger and will dominate our thinking and actions.

6. Read Proverbs 4:23. What are we encouraged to do above all else? Why?

Describe the mental picture that comes to your mind as you think of a guard.

What is the purpose of a guard?

How can you guard your heart?

How can this affect what you choose to watch on TV or movies or what you read?

In what other areas do you need to guard your mind?

7. Read Philippians 1:12-14. The apostle Paul is an example of one who chose the focus of his mind wisely. What difficult situation did he face that he could have chosen to focus on?

Upon what did Paul choose to focus?

What do you think would have happened in Paul's mind had he chosen to focus upon his imprisonment?

How do you think his focus affected his attitudes and emotions?

If Paul had focused on his imprisonment, he would have become discouraged and despondent. Instead, he focused on the good being accomplished. As a result, he was encouraged. He rejoiced in the eternal results of changed lives instead of grieving what was wrong with his situation.

8. Read Philippians 1:15-21. What sad situation could have been Paul's focus?

What was his focus?

What was the result of his focus?

What emotions would Paul have experienced if he had focused on people's wrong motives?

How does your focus affect your handling of hurtful situations?

How can your focus result in anger or joy?

CHOOSING YOUR FOCUS

Had Paul chosen to focus on the impure motives of other preachers, he could have become resentful and bitter. But as he thought about lives being changed through the gospel, he rejoiced.

In the same way, our choice of focus will determine whether we experience joy and victory or whether we are defeated by anger and bitterness. If we think about past hurts and what is wrong in others, we will never see the good in them or what God can accomplish through their lives.

9. Read Philippians 1:20-26. What did Paul expect to happen through his body (see v. 20)?

What was Paul's focus in life?

What was his focus regarding death?

How do you think Paul's focus affected his courage?

How did it affect his desire to preach the gospel?

A Closer Look at My Own Heart

10. In the first part of this chapter you were asked to list in your journal different sources of information that you fed into your mind and the amount of time you spent on each activity. You were then asked to evaluate it on the basis of whether it contributed to your sensual nature or drew you closer to God.

   Now go back to your list and ask yourself, *Which nature is my mental diet feeding most?* Ask God to show you where you need to change and how to guard your mind.

11. Read Philippians 4:8. Make a list of the things Paul tells you to think about.

   How would obedience to this verse affect what you allow to enter your mind?

Action Steps I Can Take Today

12. In your journal, record how focusing upon the attributes listed in Philippians 4:8 could change your attitudes in the following areas: criticism, resentment, fear, lust, doubt, discouragement, depression.

   On a separate piece of paper, write down each of the qualities (leave lots of space between each one) listed in Philippians 4:8. Under each quality write down things that are true upon which you *can* focus. You will probably want to go back several times and add to what you've written. Put this paper where you can see it often and be reminded to think on these things. Ask God to change your focus from evil to good.

13. Write Philippians 4:8 on a 3x5-inch card and read it several times each day. Call your memory partner at the end of the week and recite the verse to him or her without looking at your card. Reciting the verses from the previous lessons in this study will also help you retain them in your memory bank.

Remember: "God's Word in, godly actions out." You can choose to have a renewed mind! Disciplining yourself to memorize His Word is part of it.

- Five -

Step Four: Get Rid of Wrong Thoughts– Debug the Program

※

Every computer programmer recognizes the importance of testing a new program to make sure it produces accurate information. He or she does this by comparing the data produced with information already gathered through other means. If the data is incorrect or garbled, the programmer debugs the program by carefully searching for wrong commands. When the wrong commands are found, they are replaced with correct ones.

A Closer Look at the Problem

THE WAR IN THE MIND

Since our natural minds have also been programmed incorrectly, our thinking needs to be debugged. We do this by comparing our thoughts with God's Word. If the two don't line up, we are responsible to replace error with truth. But this isn't easy. In fact Scripture uses phrases like "wage war," "weapons" and "destruction of strongholds" (see 2 Corinthians 10:3-5) to describe what happens in our minds when we choose to reprogram.

1. Read 2 Corinthians 10:3-5 and describe what is happening.

    Why do you think Scripture uses the analogy of war to describe the Christian's life in the world?

    Who are your enemies?

The goal of this lesson is to help you better understand the struggle that comes as you learn to think God's thoughts instead of your own. Be alert to discover the weapons God has designed for your victory. When you use His weapons you can tear down strongholds and stand firm in Him.

A Closer Look at God's Truth

THE WAR WE ARE FIGHTING IN

2. Read Romans 7:14-25. Who are the main characters involved in this war?

    Briefly summarize the war described in these verses.

    Paul expressed his conflict with sin in verses 22 to 24. Write your own personalized paraphrase of these verses. Make it descriptive of what you feel right now.

This passage in Romans shows the intensity of the war we are fighting. In our own strength, we are unable to overcome the pull of our human natures toward sin. But God doesn't leave us in despair. Victory against the power of Satan and our sinful natures *is* possible.

3.   Read Romans 7:24—8:4. Who can give us victory (see v. 25)?

What key to winning the war is found in 8:4?

What is involved in living according to the Spirit?

Even though our enemies are strong, the Spirit of God within us is more powerful than our enemies and can give us victory. When we live "according to the Spirit," we rely upon His power. We don't attempt to overcome temptation and sin through willpower and determination. Instead, we call upon God to give us victory.

WEAPONS WE CAN USE

4.   Reread 2 Corinthians 10:3-5. Describe our spiritual weapons.

Why are weapons important to a soldier fighting a war?

Why are weapons important to you as a Christian soldier in the battle against fleshly desires and Satan's attacks?

What are these weapons able to demolish?

Verse 4 promises that our weapons have power to demolish strongholds. The word "stronghold" means "a strongly fortified place or a fortress." In biblical days, a stronghold was a heavily guarded place that was under the firm control of the army that possessed it.

What are some strongholds that Christians allow to be built in their minds?

We often allow Satan or our own human natures to build strongholds in our minds: strongholds of fear, discouragement, hatred, resentment, lust, insecurity or anger. Because these areas have been under the firm control of the enemy for a long time, we cannot remove them in our own strength. We must use God's divine weapons.

What can we do with wrong thoughts (see v. 5)?

What does it mean to "take captive every thought to make it obedient to Christ"?

How can this be accomplished?

Because we are human and live in a sinful world, unholy thoughts often pop into our minds. If we nurture them, we'll allow Satan to build strongholds in our minds that will be difficult to remove.

But we needn't allow sinful thoughts to remain and defeat us. God's Word promises that when we use divine weapons, we can take every thought captive and make it obedient to Christ. When we choose to do this, Satan will not be able to build strongholds in our minds.

The example of Jesus in the Gospel of Mark gives insight into how we can take our thoughts captive.

Hand-to-Hand Combat

5. Read Mark 8:31-33. What future events was Jesus explaining to His disciples?

What was Peter's reaction?

What was Jesus' response?

Why do you think Jesus responded so strongly to Peter's words?

Why did He speak to Peter when He rebuked Satan?

Jesus recognized that Satan was the source of the thought Peter verbalized. Knowing that the temptation to escape suffering and death was in direct opposition to His Father's will for Him, He immediately dealt with the temptation by refusing to dwell on it.

In the same way, Satan puts thoughts in our minds that oppose God's will for us. Unless we deal with them immediately, they will grow and cause us to sin.

Taking the Enemy Captive

6. Read Matthew 9:4. What does Jesus warn against?

How can entertaining thoughts be similar to entertaining guests?

When we entertain guests in our homes, we try to make them feel welcome and comfortable. In the same way, when we entertain thoughts, we allow them to feel comfortable in our minds. As we make them feel at home and feed them, they settle in more deeply.

How then do we show them to the door?

7. Read Romans 13:14. What should we refuse to think about?

8. Read Philippians 3:18—4:1. How were many professing believers living in Paul's day (see v. 18)?

What was the focus of their minds (see v. 19)?

What was Paul's focus of attention (see vv. 20,21)?

Paul wrote about these professing believers who were living as enemies of Christ and the cross with tears. Their lives dishonored Jesus because their minds were focused on earthly things. They could not live victoriously while focusing on material possessions or entertaining evil thoughts.

Neither can we. Evil thoughts produce sinful actions. We must confess them as sin, ask for cleansing and replace them with good thoughts.

Have you ever been reading and then realized that you couldn't recall what you had read? What had you done? You had allowed your mind to wander to a subject totally unrelated to what was in front of you.

Our minds are incapable of focusing on two subjects at the same time. We can change our focus from thoughts that are displeasing to God to those that are pleasing to Him!

PUTTING THE ENEMY TO DEATH

9. Read Colossians 3:1-11. Upon what should we think (see vv. 1,2)?

    What should we not think about?

    What needs to be put to death within us (see v. 5)?

    What must we get rid of (see vv. 8,9)?

    How do the characteristics in verses 5, 8 and 9 relate to the mind?

    How can these things be put to death?

To put anything to death is to deprive it of its power and its ability to control. When we use God's weapons to put evil desires and activities to death, they no longer have power to control us.

    How does verse 10 describe the new self?

Notice that the new self is *being* renewed in knowledge. The renewed mind is not an instant happening; it is a growing process. We should not get discouraged when we do not instantly achieve godly thinking in all areas of life.

10.   Read Revelation 12:11. What weapons did the victorious saints use?

How can these weapons help us overcome ungodly thoughts?

CHOOSING VICTORY

The blood of Jesus Christ, the Lamb of God, cleanses from sin. Jesus died to give us forgiveness and victory. By claiming the power of His blood and asking His help, we can overcome sinful thoughts.

The word of testimony proclaims the victory already won. Claiming God's promises enables us to recognize Satan's lies and overcome his attacks. Commitment to Jesus is crucial to victory. These saints were determined to follow Him, regardless of the cost. Because they fought Satan with divine weapons, they overcame.

A Closer Look at My Own Heart

You too can overcome Satan's lies and attacks if you use the weapons God has provided.

11.   Read Ephesians 6:10-18. Who is the source of strength (see v. 10)?

What are we told to put on?

Why?

How do verses 10-13 relate to your struggle with sinful thoughts?

How does verse 13 promise victory?

You are no match against the spiritual forces of evil if you are not clothed in the full armor of God. However, when you use His weapons, you can demolish Satan's strongholds and stand firm in the Lord.

Sinful thoughts will still come into your mind, but you don't have to let them stay. An old adage says, "You can't keep birds from flying over your head, but you don't have to let them build nests in your hair."

You *can* replace sinful thoughts with godly thoughts.

Action Steps I Can Take Today

12. Ask God to make you aware of any thought not pleasing to Him. Choose to neither feed it nor make it comfortable. Instead, with His help, take that thought "captive"—confess it as sin—and bring it to the obedience of Christ. Next, consciously choose to replace it with prayer, thanksgiving or Scripture.

13. In your journal, list thoughts you need to take captive and how you will make them obedient to Christ.

14. Memorize 2 Corinthians 10:4,5. These verses have high visual impact. Picture what is happening. Note the strong verbs. Read the verses several times aloud so you can hear it as well as see it. Doing this with your memory partner will help both of you. Also, write these verses several times to impress it more deeply in your mind. Scripture hidden in your mind has divine power to destroy the enemies that fight to gain control of your soul.

- Six -

OVERCOMING REJECTION AND GUILT

Program modification is part of every computer programmer's job. A computer programmer not only debugs programs, he or she adds to them to make them more efficient. Such program enhancement enables computers to perform additional tasks, thus increasing their productivity and usefulness.

Similarly, our natural minds need modification. Not only must we remove faulty thoughts, we must enhance our way of thinking to make us more effective for God and others.

In the previous chapters, we studied four steps for the renewal of our minds. The remaining studies give practical ways for utilizing these steps. This chapter shows how we can overcome feelings of rejection and guilt.

A Closer Look at the Problem

1. Feelings of rejection and guilt are difficult to overcome. Why do you think this is so?

Describe a time when you felt rejected by someone who was important to you.

How did it make you feel?

2. Describe a time when you did something you shouldn't have and were overcome with guilt.

Did other people contribute to your feelings of guilt? What did they say?

How did they make you feel?

Our study today takes us into Samaria where Jesus encountered a woman who lived as a social outcast. This woman understood what rejection felt like; it seems she had been rejected all her life. She also knew what it was like to be guilty. She had sinned much and she knew it. Perhaps she wondered if there were any hope for her.

And then…Jesus came through her town.

Let's see what happened.

A Closer Look at God's Truth

WHO WERE THE SAMARITANS?

Jews avoided contact with the Samaritans. After the fall of the northern kingdom of Israel, the victorious Assyrians deported the Israelites from their land, then resettled it with captives from other countries. Eventually the captives intermarried with the remaining Jews. These foreigners brought with them their own gods. Therefore, the Samaritans at the time of the New Testament embraced a religion that was a mixture of Jewish and pagan religions.

The Jewish laws at that time forbade virtually all contact between the Samaritans and Jews. When traveling between Judea and Galilee, many Jews would go the long way around—across the Jordan River and into Perea—to avoid passing through Samaria. Jesus, however, was compelled by love to go to this group of outcasts.

3. Read John 4:4-26. Why did Jesus go through Samaria (see v. 4)?

What time of day did Jesus and His disciples stop to rest (see v. 6)?

Why was the woman surprised at Jesus' request?

The sixth hour of the day was around noon. Women usually went to the well early in the morning or in the cool of early evening. Why do you think this woman was getting water during the hottest time of the day?

What effect did Jesus' request have upon her?

What kind of water did He offer her (see v. 10)?

What did He reveal about her life (see vv. 17,18)?

What feelings do you think this woman had as a result of her lifestyle?

4. Reread verses 4-26. List the ways Jesus demonstrated His acceptance of this woman.

THE PAIN OF REJECTION

This woman of Samaria must have had intense feelings of rejection and guilt. Perhaps she had been rejected as a child. As an adult she had been in five marriages, and now she was living with a man who was not her husband.

Probably the village women had also rejected her because of her lifestyle. She avoided them by coming to the well when no one was there. It hurt less to be alone than to face open rejection.

Jews treated Samaritans as outcasts and women like possessions. For a Jewish man to speak to any woman in public was unusual. To speak to a Samaritan woman was unheard of. Even after a Jew had been to market, he carefully washed himself to remove any uncleanness resulting from touching things handled by Gentiles.

In striking contrast, Jesus treated this Samaritan woman with respect and acceptance. His asking for a drink visibly demonstrated that she was a worthwhile human being. He offered her living water, explained true worship and revealed Himself as the Messiah.

5. Read John 4:27-30. What did the woman do after their conversation (see vv. 28-30)?

How beautiful to see the difference in this woman who had known so much failure. The accepting love of Jesus reached out to her and she was changed. This woman who would not go to the well when the other women were there hurried to town to tell everyone she could about Jesus.

6. Read John 4:39-42. What resulted from the woman's testimony?

What does Jesus' encounter with the woman at the well tell you about His accepting love?

Jesus reached out to this woman right where she was. He looked beyond her sin to her potential and engulfed her in His accepting and forgiving love. When the realization of His love touched her, she saw herself as God saw her and was able to reach out to others with the good news of Jesus Christ. Before she had been powerless to change the behavior that probably contributed to the rejection she faced; now she was able to change the behavior that had previously turned others away.

7.   Read Romans 15:7. What does this verse tell us that Jesus has done?

8.   Read Isaiah 41:9,10. Fill in the blanks from the last part of verse 9 (*NIV*):

"I have _____ you and have
not _____ you."

What does God promise to those He has chosen (see v. 10)?

CHOOSING ACCEPTANCE RATHER THAN REJECTION

Often those who struggle most with rejection are those who have experienced what they perceived as rejection in their childhood. The one who sees him- or herself as unacceptable begins to expect it and even assumes it in actions that were never intended to convey rejection. That person even sees rejection coming from God. This feeling of rejection hinders a person from responding to God's love and to other people, and intensifies the problem. Because of the intense pain, he or she builds protective walls around him- or herself.

To overcome feelings of rejection, we must allow God's Holy Spirit to reprogram our thinking. Rejecting the negative self-talk that says, *I'm no good; therefore, no one will accept me,* and accepting God's Words, "I have chosen you and have not rejected you" (Isaiah 41:9) will help us understand that rejection from others does not make us worthless.

We must choose to replace false statements with truth. God says that He accepts us; therefore, we can believe Him and praise Him for loving us just the way we are.

Sometimes feelings of rejection come because we have been rejected by others. However, human love can never meet our deepest need. Only God is able to love with a perfect love. Often those who have not experienced an accepting love find it difficult to love others. A vicious cycle has begun, a cycle that only God can break.

To overcome this devastation of rejection, we need to forgive those who have hurt us and ask God to forgive us for our bitterness. When we bless the people that we once shut out of our lives with prayers, words and deeds, we ourselves are strengthened.

A Closer Look at My Own Heart

CHOOSING FREEDOM RATHER THAN GUILT

9. Read Romans 8:1-4. Sometimes we feel rejected because we also feel guilty. When we struggle with guilt, we see ourselves as unworthy of anyone's accepting love. What is promised to those who are in Christ Jesus (see v. 1)?

What results in our lives when we accept Jesus as Lord?

Explain what you think is meant by the phrase "that the righteous requirements of the law might be fully met in us" (v. 4).

The law requires perfect obedience. But we are no longer under the law. When Jesus became a sin offering for us, He paid the penalty for all our sin. Through His death on the cross, He has satisfied all the demands of the law. When we accept Him as Savior, He takes our sins and exchanges them for His righteousness. We no longer need to feel guilty, because He has forgiven us.

If we sin after receiving salvation, we are told to confess and turn from that sin. The moment we do, we are freed from guilt.

10. Read 1 John 1:9. What is promised to those who confess sin?

How does knowing that you are forgiven and cleansed make you feel?

Action Steps I Can Take Today

This lesson shows that God accepts and forgives you. He has set you free from the anguish of guilt and rejection. In contrast, Satan bombards you with suggestions of guilt and worthlessness. You can gain victory over his deception by applying the following four steps for renewing your mind.

> *Step One: Draw near to God—connect to the power source.* Spend time in prayer today asking God to help you grasp hold of the reality of His love. Thank Him that He accepts you even with your weaknesses and failures. Confess any sins that need His forgiveness. Thank Him that you are forgiven and are holy in His sight.

> *Step Two: Use God's Word—your instruction manual.* God's Word is truth and He says you are accepted, forgiven, holy and blameless. Find one or two Scripture verses which proclaim these truths. Copy these on 3x5-inch cards and place them where you will see them often. Meditate upon the acceptance and forgiveness that is yours. Memorize these verses and claim them as your own.

> *Step Three: Think on good things—input valid data.* Think about the righteousness of Jesus. In your journal, write down what you think it means to receive His righteousness. List the past, present and

future blessings that are available to you because you have the righteousness of Christ.

Step Four: Get rid of wrong thoughts—debug the program. Each time you have a thought of rejection or guilt this week, write it in your journal. Combat it with a Scripture verse, a prayer or a praise. You can do this by:

1. Confessing sin and asking for forgiveness immediately. Believe that forgiveness is yours.
2. Instead of dwelling on the condemning thought, praise God for His forgiveness. Praise God that He lovingly accepts you just as you are.
3. Record in your journal how you took that thought captive and made it obedient to Christ.

11. Write Isaiah 41:9,10 on a 3x5-inch card. On the back of the card, write a praise song to God for the promises He has given you in these verses. Read the verse each day and sing your praise song out loud.

12. Check in often with your memory partner. Continue to do this until you have memorized the verses you selected in Step Two and/or Isaiah 41:9,10.

Seven

OVERCOMING FEAR AND WORRY

One procedure computer programmers often use is a loop—a set of instructions that performs repetitious tasks. The loop does its job as many times as necessary, then returns to the main body of the program.

If, however, the programmer writes the code incorrectly, the program can become stuck in the loop. The computer repeats the instructions until it comes to a standstill and is unable to perform other functions. To correct the program, the programmer must identify and reprogram the faulty code.

A Closer Look at the Problem

In many ways, fear and worry affect us like programs that have gone into loops. Our minds go over and over the same fears. They paralyze our thinking and make us unable to function properly. Psychologists call this "negative-loop thinking."

We may have trouble sleeping because we can't turn our thoughts off. A fear awakens us and the next thing we know we are rehearsing everything that might happen. During the day it may be hard to concentrate on our work. Even paying attention to the needs of our family can become difficult or even impossible.

In chapter six we were given four steps to help us overcome rejection and guilt and renew our minds. In this chapter we will study the crisis that faced King Jehoshaphat. We will see how these same four steps can be applied in the areas of fear and worry. We will also look closely at the spies who entered the Promised Land and brought back a negative report. Instead of focusing on God they were overcome by fear.

Let's briefly review the steps that brought victory to King Jehoshaphat. First, draw near to God. Secondly, read and memorize Scripture. Thirdly, focus on good things. Fourthly, get rid of wrong thoughts and replace them with godly ones.

God has something better for us than negative-loop thinking. Our minds can be reprogrammed to overcome fear and worry.

A Closer Look at God's Truth

A GODLY KIND OF FEAR

There are two kinds of fears—wholesome and unhealthy. Second Chronicles 20:1-13 is an exciting illustration of what can happen in a situation when a wholesome fear spurred a king and his people to action.

1. Read 2 Chronicles 20:1-13. Describe the situation that faced King Jehoshaphat.

    What was there about this situation that could have caused him to panic?

    What word from verse 3 describes his emotions?

    Do you think the people of Judah had a valid reason to fear? Give reasons for your answer.

Fear is intended to spur us into action in treacherous situations. If we did not have a wholesome fear, we would take no protective actions when danger strikes. In contrast, unhealthy fear causes panic that makes us unable to cope.

2. What two actions did Jehoshaphat take because of the crisis?

    How did the people respond?

    As Jehoshaphat prayed, he proclaimed the power of God. List phrases from verses 6 to 9 which emphasize God's might.

    Which verse reminds God of His promise to Israel?

    What phrase from verse 12 shows the severity of the problem?

    What key to overcoming fear is found in verse 12?

3. Reread 2 Chronicles 20:1-13. As you do, keep in mind the four steps for renewing your mind. Either in the space below, or in your journal, indicate how Jehoshaphat and his people put each step into practice as they faced this frightening situation.

The king and the people of Judah first drew near to God with prayer and fasting. They claimed His promises. They focused on His power, rather than the power of the enemy. They took their thoughts of worry and fear captive and fixed their eyes on God to see what He would do.

4. Read 2 Chronicles 20:14-19. List the assurances God gave them in verses 15-17:

    What was their response to God's promises (see vv. 18,19)?

    Why do you think they responded this way?

As they drew near to God, He strengthened them and promised deliverance. In faith, they claimed His promises. Although the dangerous situation had not changed, they experienced the peace and joy that comes through total trust in God.

5. Read 2 Chronicles 20:20-30. How did Jehoshaphat encourage his people (see v. 20)?

    Then what did he do?

    What happened as they sang and praised?

    How can praise to God help you overcome fear?

Praising God for His goodness and greatness helps us fix our "eyes"—our minds—on God and reminds us of His absolute power in any difficult situation. When we praise Him, we acknowledge His control.

6.   How were the invading armies defeated (see v. 23)?

     Who won the battle?

God turned a potentially devastating situation into good for these people who trusted Him. Because they cried out to Him for help, He overcame the fears that could have immobilized them. They listened to truth about who God was, then marched into battle with praise on their lips.

FEAR THAT PARALYZES AND DESTROYS

This next passage is a tragic example of how fear cripples God's people and leads to disobedience. As you study, be on the look out for evidences of the negative-loop thinking that we discussed earlier. Notice how, instead of taking God at His word, the Israelites lost their focus by paying too much attention to what they saw with their eyes and thought with their minds.

7.   Read Numbers 13:1-3. What did the Lord tell Moses to do?

     What did God promise to give the Israelites?

8.   Read Numbers 13:26-33. What had the ten spies chosen as their focus?

     What did their fear lead them to do (see v. 32)?

How was Caleb's report different from that of the other spies (see v. 30)?

9. Read Numbers 14:1-12. How did the people of Israel respond to these reports?

How does this Scripture illustrate the detrimental effect of fear?

Joshua and Caleb tried to persuade the Israelites to abandon their fears and move forward into the Promised Land. What phrases show the reason for their confidence (see vv. 8,9)?

Why do you think Joshua and Caleb's reactions contrasted with those of the other spies?

How did God view the fear and disobedience of the people?

10. Read Mark 4:40. How did Jesus view His disciples' fear in this verse?

How is unbelief related to fear?

How does fear show contempt for God?

11. Read about the boy who needed healing in Mark 9:14-24. How did the boy's father handle his unbelief?

What actions had he already taken, despite his unbelief, that demonstrated faith (vv. 17,18)?

Fear and worry indicate that we are not trusting the Lord to work out difficult situations. The Israelites did not enter the land because they did not believe that God would keep His promises.

How is the father in Mark 9 a good example in confessing unbelief?

Read verses 25-27. What was the result?

12. Read Numbers 14:26-38. What were the consequences of the Israelites' fear?

How did God reward the faith of Joshua and Caleb (see v. 38)?

13. Compare the account of the Israelites' refusal to believe God and enter Canaan with the account of Judah's victory in the Valley of Beracah.

Israel's Defeat—The Spies   Judah's Victory—Jehoshaphat

What were the key differences in the way both groups handled fear?

Describe ways that fear can keep you from obeying God.

A Closer Look at My Own Heart

14. Read Philippians 4:6-9. Answer the following questions, then personalize the verses into a prayer for you to pray and a promise for you to claim.

What are you told not to be anxious about?

What are you to do instead?

What will result?

———∽∾∽———

A prayer for you to pray, from your heart to His heart,
A promise for you to claim, from His heart to yours:

My Prayer:

My Promise:

Action Steps I Can Take Today

15. God does not want you to be anxious about anything. By using the following four steps for the renewal of the mind, you can overcome fear and worry.

Step One: Draw near to God—connect to the power source. Spend time in prayer today, confessing your fears and worries. Ask Him to take control of your difficult situations and help you overcome your fears.

Step Two: Use God's Word—your instruction manual. Like Jehoshaphat and his men, remind God of His promises. Find one or two Scripture verses that proclaim His trustworthiness. Write them in your journal and on 3x5-inch cards and place them where you will see them often. Memorize them, meditate upon them and claim them.

Step Three: Think on good things—input valid data. In your journal, list ways God proved His faithfulness to Jehoshaphat and the people of Judah. Record times in the past when the Lord showed His trustworthiness to you in frightening situations. Every day this week, thank God for His faithfulness to you.

Step Four: Get rid of wrong thoughts—debug the program. Each time you have a fearful or worrisome thought this week, note it in your journal. Replace that thought with prayer for the situation and thanksgiving that God is worthy of your trust. Now record how you substituted prayer and praise for fear and worry.

16. Write Philippians 4:6,7 on a 3x5-inch card. Turn the card over. On the back draw a heart in the center of the card. Inside the heart, write:

> Prayer
> Petition
> Requests

Create a border of peace encircling the heart—illustrate peace in whatever way is meaningful to you. How does it make you feel to see a visual illustration of God's peace protecting your mind and heart?

Share your visual illustration with your memory partner. Spend time praying together for one another's petitions and requests.

- Eight -

OVERCOMING DISCOURAGEMENT

———⊷ɷ⊷———

In chapters six and seven we learned how to renew our minds in our struggles against rejection and guilt and against fear and worry. This chapter will help us in our struggle against discouragement.

Even though discouragement is not part of God's plan, it often overcomes believers in their walk with God. Not only does it rob believers of God's blessings, it robs those closest to them of blessings as well.

This chapter shows how we can reprogram our minds to overcome discouragement and experience God's hope.

A Closer Look at the Problem

1. Check the sentences that describe what you have experienced this past year:

    ❑   There have been times when I have wondered if God cares about my problems.
    ❑   I have been tempted to stop praying about a need because it seems to do no good.

❑   I have felt like quitting Christian work because I have seen so few
     results.
❑   I have felt like giving up on studying the Bible because every time I
     do, something happens to push it out of my schedule.

2.   If you checked even one of the above sentences, you understand some-
     thing of the power of discouragement. Are there other situations that
     make you discouraged? List some of them:

Probably most Christians have struggled with discouragement at some time,
but God's plan is that we be encouraged to live in the fullness Jesus came to
give.

    The apostle Paul faced great difficulties in his ministry which could have
made him discouraged. Our study will show how he, through the power of the
Holy Spirit, used the four steps to renewal of the mind to gain victory and
encouragement.

    These steps are for us, too. Let's read and study and learn more about the
hope we can experience when we focus on Christ Jesus.

A Closer Look at God's Truth

FOCUSING ON GOD'S POWER

3.   Read 2 Corinthians 4:5-12. What was Paul's source of power?

     List words and phrases that describe his difficult circumstances (see vv. 8,9):

List phrases describing victory over those situations:

Did Paul have reason for discouragement? Why or why not?

Christians get discouraged when they focus on problems rather than on the power of God. Paul, however, rejoiced that the Lord used his struggles to accomplish good. Instead of focusing on destruction, he focused upon the eternal life that would be his and that was being brought forth in others.

4.   Read 2 Corinthians 4:13-18. What was Paul's focus of attention (see v. 14)?

What phrase indicates Paul's lack of discouragement?

What key to overcoming discouragement is found in verse 16?

Paul relied upon God's all-surpassing power at work in his life (see v. 7). He knew that he could not endure hardships by himself. Only when he drew into God's presence daily was he empowered and renewed. The same is true for us.

Why is it important that we be renewed daily?

How can this be accomplished?

5.   Reread 2 Corinthians 4:17,18. How did Paul refer to his troubles (see v. 17)?

What were these troubles achieving for him?

Upon what did he choose to focus?

Why did he choose that focus?

Compare verse 17 to 2 Corinthians 11:23-29. Why do you think Paul could refer to such trials as "light and momentary"?

How did his choice of focus affect his attitude?

What would have resulted if he had focused on this life?

Because Paul focused on God's promises of eternal life and glory, his trials faded in importance. Satan was unable to defeat him through discouragement because he was daily being renewed in God's presence. Paul had chosen to fix his eyes upon heavenly things.

6.   Read 2 Corinthians 1:3-11. How is God described in verse 3?

What does He do for us in our troubles?

When we struggle with discouragement, we often pretend that all is well. We may not want to burden people or want others to think we are unspiritual. However, behind our cheerful exteriors, our hearts may be breaking.

We can always be honest with God. We can tell Him our confusion and discouragements and He is always willing to comfort and encourage.

What does God's comfort enable us to do (see v. 4)?

List phrases from verses 4-7 which emphasize Paul's focus upon the good being accomplished in his trials:

BELIEVERS ENCOURAGING BELIEVERS

7. When Paul wrote to the church at Rome, he identified another important source of encouragement. Read Romans 1:11,12. What would result from Paul's visit to the Roman believers?

God planned that we be involved in churches and groups where we can encourage one another in our struggles without fear of condemnation or disapproval. Often, the people who encourage us the most are those who have gone through similar trials. As they honestly share how God comforted them in their struggles, we receive hope for ours. There is no greater comfort than the comfort they receive from God and then pass on to us.

Share a time when someone comforted you with the comfort he or she received from God. How did his or her comfort encourage you?

How have you been able to share that comfort with someone else?

8. Reread 2 Corinthians 1:8-11. Describe briefly the sufferings Paul endured (see v. 8).

How does verse 9 emphasize the severity of his situation?

Why did God allow this trial to occur (see v. 9)?

What aspects of God's power did Paul focus upon (see vv. 9,10)?

What phrases show Paul's lack of discouragement (see vv. 10,11)?

Reread 2 Corinthians 1:3-11 and list all the good results of his difficulties.

Too often, we get discouraged because we fail to see God's purposes in difficult situations. It helps to realize that He allows us to go through trials to strengthen and mature us, and make us a blessing to others.

9. Read 1 Corinthians 16:8,9. Why did Paul choose to stay in Ephesus?

What difficult experience was he facing?

EXPERIENCING OPPOSITION

In this life, we'll always have problems. Satan especially opposes us if we are doing something worthwhile for the Lord. He tells us we are wasting our time and that we won't see any lasting results. If we have sinned, he whispers that God can't possibly use us again.

We should not only recognize the lies, but expect the opposition. Actually, we should be encouraged by it. In a football game, the opponents never tackle people sitting on the benches. They go after the quarterback or the receivers—the ones making the scores.

In the same way, Satan is not concerned about Christians sitting on the side-lines who never enter the battle. However, if we throw ourselves wholeheartedly into Christian service, he'll fight us with every weapon he can muster. We must not let his weapons overwhelm us with discouragement. Instead, let's be encouraged. God says we will reap a harvest if we don't give up.

A Closer Look at My Own Heart

10. Think back to a difficult time in your life. Ask God to show you the good that was accomplished in you and in others. Record your thoughts in your journal, then thank Him that He is working to bring growth and greater ministry into your life.

11. What keys to overcoming discouragement are found in the following passages?

Psalm 119:28

Hebrews 11:24-28

Hebrews 12:2,3

12. What is promised in the following verses?

1 Corinthians 15:58

Galatians 6:9,10

Hebrews 6:10

James 1:12

1 Peter 5:10

Does one of these verses speak to your need for encouragement? Write it in your journal and claim it as a promise from God's heart to yours.

Action Steps I Can Take Today

13. Although Satan will bombard you with discouraging thoughts, God does not want you to be cast down. By using the four steps for the renewal of the mind, you can overcome discouragement.

    Step One: Draw near to God—connect to the power source. Ask God to show you areas of discouragement that are keeping you from experiencing the hope and joy He wants you to have. Record these in your journal, then confess them to Him and ask for His encouragement and strength. Write the words to your prayer in your journal.

    Step Two: Use God's Word—your instruction manual. Nothing encourages like the Word of God. Find a promise in Scripture that speaks to your specific need for encouragement. Write it in your journal, then on a 3x5-inch card and place it where you can see it often. Memorize the verse and thank God that He keeps His promises.

Step Three: Think on good things—input valid data. Ask God to show you the good being accomplished through your difficulties. Record what He reveals to you. Thank Him for the spiritual growth and expanded ministry that He is bringing into your life through difficulties. Record your words of praise.

Step Four: Get rid of wrong thoughts—debug the program. Determine to take discouraging thoughts captive to the obedience of Jesus. Ask Him to make you especially aware of each one as it occurs, then replace each negative thought with a thanksgiving or a promise from Scripture. In your journal, record how you made each discouraging thought obedient to Jesus. Choose to praise Him, regardless of your feelings.

14. Share the verse you wrote on your card with your memory partner. Ask him or her to pray for you as you sort through Satan's lies and claim God's promises for your life. Take time to pray with one another. Continue to review together the verses you learned earlier in this study.

- Nine -

OVERCOMING DISOBEDIENCE

In chapters two through five we studied key verses to learn essential steps in renewing our minds and helping us acquire the mind of Christ. In chapters six through eight, we learned how to apply these steps in our struggles in difficult areas—rejection, guilt, fear, worry and discouragement.

But there's more. Perhaps more than anything, we simply need to learn to obey our Lord.

A Closer Look at the Problem

As committed believers, we desire to exalt Jesus. Unfortunately, we cannot do that if we disobey Him. Our problem is that, even though we want to obey, we often fail to do so because our minds are still controlled by our old natures. Instead of victory, we expect and accept defeat.

This chapter shows how the Holy Spirit can reprogram our thinking to enable us to live in obedient surrender to God's will. It will help you understand how you can be obedient to the call of God on your life.

A Closer Look at God's Truth

AN OBEDIENT MAN OF GOD

Abraham is an example of a believer who obeyed the Lord. As you study these passages, be alert to conditions which led to his obedient responses.

1. Read Genesis 12:1-8. What did the Lord tell Abraham to do (see v. 1)?

    What did God promise Abraham (see vv. 2,3)?

    How did Abraham respond to the Lord's directions (see v. 4)?

    What did God promise Abraham after he arrived in Canaan?

    How would you describe Abraham's relationship with God?

    How did his trust influence his actions?

2. Read Hebrews 11:8-10. What quality enabled Abraham to obey (see vv. 8,9)?

    What was the focus of Abraham's mind (see v. 10)?

How did the focus of his mind affect his willingness to obey?

Probably one of the chief causes of disobedience is our tendency to focus on earthly values and rewards instead of heavenly rewards. Concentrating on problems and desires of this world, we lose sight of God's best. Abraham, however, obeyed because he looked forward to eternal rewards.

3. Read Genesis 17:9-11,15-27. What did God ask Abraham to do as a sign of the covenant between them?

What did God promise Abraham (see v. 16)?

What did God promise regarding Isaac (see vv. 19-21)?

What do verses 23-27 reveal about Abraham's response to God's command?

These verses portray a close, trusting relationship between Abraham and God. When God spoke, Abraham listened and obeyed. As they talked and spent time together, Abraham's faith grew. They were friends. Abraham knew he could trust God to keep His promises.

4. Read Genesis 21:1-5. List phrases that indicate God kept His promise.

How did the birth of Isaac affect Abraham's trust in God?

One of the greatest truths we can learn is that God always keeps His promises. God did exactly what He said He would do for Abraham. He can be trusted to keep His promises, right down to the very last detail.

5. Read Hebrews 11:11. What enabled Abraham and Sarah to become parents in their old age?

What phrase shows their view of God?

Abraham and the people of faith described in Hebrews 11 believed in the faithfulness of God, whether they could literally see the fulfillment of His promises or not. Their faith did not depend on outward circumstances, but on the trustworthiness of a mighty God. God asks us, too, to trust His promises even when we cannot see their fulfillment in our lifetimes.

6. Read Genesis 22:1-14. What did God ask Abraham to do (see v. 2)?

What thoughts and feelings do you think Abraham experienced as a result of this request?

How did this command seem to contradict God's promise in Genesis 17:19?

There is probably no command ever given to a man that would have been more difficult to obey than this one. God had promised Abraham a child; He had promised that He would establish His covenant with Isaac and his descendants.

The child of promise had been born, but now it seemed that God was going back on His promise. If Isaac were to die on that mountain, there would be no descendants. Could God still be trusted to keep His word?

How is verse 5 an indication of Abraham's trust in God's promises?

How does verse 8 show Abraham's continued trust in God?

How did God prove Himself faithful and trustworthy?

How is this story similar to the provision God made at Calvary through the death of Jesus?

How do both stories demonstrate the trustworthiness of God?

God provided a ram to take Isaac's place upon the altar of sacrifice. In the same way, He provided Jesus as the perfect Lamb of God to die in our place. In one tremendous sacrifice of love, Jesus paid the penalty for our sin. We choose whether or not we will accept or reject the provision God made through Jesus Christ. Such a loving God deserves our trusting obedience.

7. Read Hebrews 11:17-19. What had Abraham done with God's promises (see v. 17)?

What does verse 19 reveal regarding Abraham's focus?

How did Abraham believe God would keep His promises if Isaac were killed as a sacrifice?

How did Abraham's focus affect his ability to obey?

How does your focus affect your obedience?

Abraham obeyed because he was fully convinced that a trustworthy God would keep His promises. The Lord also asks us to trust Him enough to respond in obedience.

CHOOSING TO OBEY
Our view of the power of sin will influence our obedience.

8. Read Romans 6:11-23. How should we think of ourselves (see v. 11)?

List phrases that indicate sin is a choice. Give the verses.

List phrases that show sin does not have power over us.

How will thinking of yourself as dead to sin affect your actions?

What happens if you see yourself as powerless to overcome sin?

God asks us to be holy, just as He is holy. However, attempting to fight sin by trying to be good always ends in failure. Obedience can seem to be an impossible goal, but it isn't. God has given us the power of the Holy Spirit within us to enable us to live the holy life He has commanded. Victory is possible because

Jesus broke the power of sin on the cross. When we acknowledge our weakness and ask God for His power to defeat sin in our lives we are victorious.

9. Read 1 Corinthians 10:13. What does God promise us?

In light of God's promise in this verse, why do so many of us continue to sin?

What will you choose to do the next time you are faced with a temptation?

A Closer Look at My Own Heart

10. A verse for you to ponder: Read 2 Timothy 2:20,21. What does God promise when you choose to allow Him to cleanse you?

God wants to use you as an instrument in His kingdom, but He will not pour the fullness of His Holy Spirit into a dirty vessel. God will use you only if you obey Him.

11. A prayer for you:

Lord, more than anything I long to please you. Cleanse me.

Continue to teach me how to firmly connect to You as my source of power for change. Instill within me a strong determination to put Your Word into my mind so that I might think Your thoughts. Teach me to think on the things that draw me closer to You.

Show me how to apply Your truths to overcome any feelings of rejection or guilt that I might still need to deal with. Lead me away from fears and worries and into Your peace. Keep me from discouragement. Above all, lead me into the path of obedience. Only then will I be a cleansed vessel, useful to You, my Master, prepared for every good work. In Jesus' name, amen.

Action Steps I Can Take Today

12.   The following steps will help you become His obedient child.

Step One: Draw near to God—connect to the power source. Obedience is the result of coming into God's presence and receiving His strength. Will you, right now, ask God to show you any area of disobedience in your life?

Will you…

- ❏ Confess each as sin and acknowledge your inability to obey in your own strength?
- ❏ Ask Him for His power to overcome the sin He has revealed?
- ❏ Spend time with Him each day this week?
- ❏ Ask Him to increase your desire and willingness to obey?

Step Two: Use God's Word—your instruction manual. When Abraham focused on God's promises, he wanted to obey God. Find several promises in Scripture for those who are obedient, also a passage that promises victory over sin. Write them in your journal and on a 3x5-inch card, then place them where you can see them often. Memorize and meditate upon each one. Claim them as your own.

Consistent study is also an important key to being able to live in obedience. Choosing to daily feed upon God's Word means you can be continually strengthened by it.

Step Three: Think on good things—input valid data. Carefully evaluate what you put into your mind. Do the TV programs you watch and the books you read help you to overcome temptation? Or do they lead you to greater temptation? Do they feed your spiritual nature or your sinful nature? What changes can you make to better guard your mind? Record those changes in your journal.

Step Four: Get rid of wrong thoughts—debug the program. Ask God to help you quickly identify thoughts that produce disobedience. Choose to refuse to entertain or feed them.

Will you…
- ❑ Choose now to replace those thoughts with prayer, asking God for His victory?
- ❑ Acknowledge your weakness to overcome in your own strength, but claim the power of God that is available in Christ Jesus?
- ❑ Write in your journal how you made your thoughts obedient to Him?

12. Make a commitment to continue to memorize God's Word. Write your verses on 3x5-inch cards. Keep them with you, pull them out and review them in spare moments. Newly memorized verses need to be read daily, then weekly and monthly—a few times each day. Memorization takes repetition and review.

13. As you complete this Bible study, remember this: The Holy Spirit wants to renew your mind and build the attitudes of Christ into your thinking. He wants to make you holy, a person set apart for His purpose. He wants you to allow His Word to mold you into the image of Jesus.

"If a man cleanses himself…he will be an instrument for noble purposes, made holy, useful to the Master and prepared to do any good work."
2 Timothy 2:21

What Is Aglow International?

From one nation to 135 worldwide...
From one fellowship to over 3,300...
From 100 women to more than 2 million...

Aglow International has experienced phenomenal growth since
its inception 30 years ago. In 1967, four women from the state
of Washington prayed for a way to reach out to other Christian
women in simple fellowship, free from denominational boundaries.

The first meeting held in Seattle, Washington, USA, drew more
than 100 women to a local hotel. From that modest beginning,
Aglow International has become one of the largest intercultural,
interdenominational women's organizations in the world.

Each month, Aglow touches the lives of an estimated two million
women on six continents through local fellowship meetings,
Bible studies, support groups, retreats, conferences and various
outreaches. From the inner city to the upper echelons, from the
woman next door to the corporate executive, Aglow seeks to
minister to the felt needs of women around the world.

Christian women find Aglow a "safe place" to grow spiritually
and begin to discover and use the gifts, talents and abilities God
has given them. Aglow offers excellent leadership training and
varied opportunities to develop those leadership skills.

Undergirding the evangelistic thrust of the ministry is an empha-
sis on prayer, which has led to an active prayer network linking
six continents. The vast prayer power available through Aglow
women around the world is being used by God to influence
countless lives in families, communities, cities and nations.

Aglow's Mission Statement

Our mission is to lead women to Jesus Christ and provide opportunity for Christian women to grow in their faith and minister to others.

—◆◇◇◆—

Aglow's Continuing Focus...

- To reconcile woman to her womanhood as God designed. To strengthen and empower her to fulfill the unfolding plan of God as He brings restoration to the male/female relationship, which is the foundation of the home, the church and the community.
- To love women of all cultures with a special focus on Muslim women.
- To reach out to every strata of society, from inner cities to isolated outposts to our own neighborhoods, with very practical and tangible expressions of the love of Jesus.

—◆◇◇◆—

Gospel Light and Aglow International present an important new series of Bible studies for use in small groups. The first two studies in the Aglow Bible Study Series, **Shame: Thief of Intimacy** *and* **Keys to Contentment**, *are available through Gospel Light. Look for these and others in the Aglow Bible Study Series including* **Fashioned for Intimacy Study Guide**, *companion to the book* **Fashioned for Intimacy**, **Building Better Relationships** *and* **God's Character**. *For information about these and other outstanding Bible study resources from Aglow, call us at 1-800-793-8126.*

Aglow Ministers In...

Albania, Angola, Anguilla, Antigua, Argentina, Aruba, Australia, Austria, Bahamas, Barbados, Belgium, Belize, Benin, Bermuda, Bolivia, Botswana, Brazil, British Virgin Islands, Bulgaria, Burkina Faso, Cameroon, Canada, Cayman Islands, Chile, China, Colombia, Congo (Rep. of), Congo (Dem. Rep. of), Costa Rica, Côte d'Ivoire, Cuba, Curaçao, Czech Republic, Denmark, Djibouti, Dominica, Dominican Republic, Ecuador, Egypt, El Salvador, England, Equatorial Guinea, Estonia, Ethiopia, Faroe Islands, Fiji, Finland, France, Gabon, the Gambia, Germany, Ghana, Greece, Grenada, Guam, Guatemala, Guinea, Guyana, Haiti, Honduras, Hungary, Iceland, India, Indonesia, Ireland, Israel, Jamaica, Japan, Kazakstan, Kenya, Korea, Kyrgyzstan, Latvia, Malawi, Malaysia, Mali, Mauritius, Mexico, Fed. States of Micronesia, Mongolia, Mozambique, Myanmar, Nepal, Netherlands, Papua New Guinea, New Zealand, Nicaragua, Niger, Nigeria, Norway, Oman, Pakistan, Panama, Peru, Philippines, Portugal, Puerto Rico, Romania, Russia, Rwanda, Samoa (American), Samoa (Western), Scotland, Senegal, Sierra Leone, Singapore, South Africa, Spain, Sri Lanka, St. Kitts, St. Lucia, St. Maartan, St. Vincent, Sudan, Suriname, Sweden, Switzerland, Tajikistan, Tanzania, Thailand, Togo, Tonga, Trinidad/ Tobago, Turks & Caicos Islands, Uganda, Ukraine, United States, U.S. Virgin Islands, Uruguay, Uzbekistan, Venezuela, Vietnam, Wales, Yugoslavia, Zambia, Zimbabwe, plus one extremely restricted 10/40 Window nation.

How do I find my nearest Aglow Fellowship? Call or write us at:

AGLOW
INTERNATIONAL

P.O. Box 1749, Edmonds, WA 98020-1749
Phone: (425) 775-7282 or 1-800-755-2456
Fax: (425) 778-9615   E-mail: aglow@aglow.org
Web site: http://www.aglow.org/

The Aglow Bible Study Series

Shame:
Thief of Intimacy
Marie Powers

Powers exposes the characteristics, contributors, and the cure for this emotion that affects women, knowingly or unknowingly, throughout the world.

Paperback • $6.99
ISBN 08307.21290
Available April 1998

Keys to
Contentment
Sharon A. Steele

Journey through this study of Paul's life and teachings in his letter to the Philippians and learn how to find the contentment and abundant, joyous life that Jesus promised.

Paperback • $6.99
ISBN 08307.21304
Available April 1998

Building Better
Relationships
Bobbie Yagel

Use the Scriptures to build successful relationships with your loved ones, friends and neighbors, and learn how to handle confrontations and know when and how to seek forgiveness.

Paperback • $6.99
ISBN 08307.21320
Available July 1998

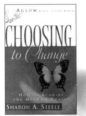

Choosing
to Change
Sharon A. Steele

Overcome rejection, guilt, fear, worry, discouragement and disobedience with the help of four essential steps to renew your mind and transform your life according to Christ.

Paperback • $6.99
ISBN 08307.21312
Available July 1998

Fashioned for Intimacy
Jane Hansen
with Marie Powers

Jane Hansen, international president of Aglow International, describes God's original design for men and women.

Hardcover • $17.99
ISBN 08307.20669
Available now

More titles in the *Aglow Bible Study Series* are coming soon: two in October 1998 and two in January 1999.

Gospel Light

Ask for these resources at your local Christian Bookstore.

Let Jane Hansen Lead Your Next Study

Jane Hansen describes the true biblical relationship God yearns to have with each of us. Discover God's original plan for intimacy, and how men and women can be reconciled to Him and each other.

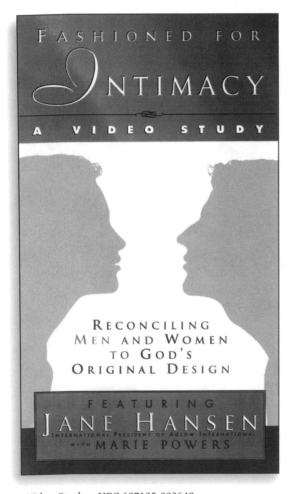

"Fashioned for Intimacy will radically impact the Body of Christ! I highly recommend it to both men and women."
—*Dutch Sheets*
Pastor of Springs Harvest Fellowship
Colorado Springs, CO

"In a time when there is a massive assault coming against the family, resources like this one by Jane Hansen will help to turn the tide of the battle. This is must reading for men and women alike."
—*Rick Joyner*
Morningstar Publications and Ministries

Video Study • UPC 607135.003649

Available at your local Christian bookstore.

Gospel Light